Mom's Life Story Journal

Mom's Life Story *journal*

Guided Prompts to Capture Your
Memories and Share Stories

KRISTEN FOGLE

ROCKRIDGE
PRESS

THIS JOURNAL BELONGS TO:

CONTENTS

INTRODUCTION

Hi, my name is Kristen, and I'm a writer.

I've written professionally since 2006, and I have run a writing center for almost 10 years. But that's just my story. I think a writer is anyone who puts pen to paper. It's that simple. And that's where you come in!

Each of us has an important story to tell—a story about where we come from, where we've been, and where we would like to go. Each area is wholly unique and can be a lot of fun to explore. You might have moments that come to you right away, or as you wade in a little deeper, you might stumble upon things you haven't remembered in years. Many of our stories are incredibly enlightening; others are just downright entertaining. Although the goal here isn't to unearth triggering or traumatic memories, there may be some painful ones; feel free to explore these or skip over them—you choose.

So many people that come to our writing center feel overwhelmed or don't know where to start. Maybe you feel that way, too. Everyone does at some point—sometimes I feel that way! But there's an easy solution. Take it one word and one sentence at a time. You're just aiming to put words down. (It's like the saying "Done is better than perfect.") By telling our tales, even imperfectly, we really learn about ourselves. Also, if you share this book after completing it, this book can be an incredible resource—a keepsake for future generations.

You chose (or were gifted) this book because you're a mom. As a mom to an almost three-year-old, I can attest that "mom-ing" is hard, amazing, nerve-racking, frustrating, illuminating, fulfilling—and that's just in one hour. Rearing a child is full of so many conflicting emotions, for sure; but even just becoming a mom can be, too. For those of you who have endured difficult adoption processes or IVF or custody battles, I see you. For those moms who have miscarried, I've been you. However you got here, I hope you felt held and seen; your story is worthy. You're worthy.

Now, let's get to the writing. The rules are . . . that there are no rules! You can go chapter by chapter if you'd like, which takes you through chronological and thematic writing prompts. Invite yourself to skip past, go back to, or change words in prompts as you wish. Feel free to write in the book or use a journal or notebook to record your answers.

Writing is just like parenting—there is no one right way to do it. Just get comfortable. Pour yourself a cold one or heat up something delicious. This is your time, your story to savor and share.

All About Me

DATE

MY NAME

MY AGE

I LIVE IN

MY FAMILY CONSISTS OF

WHAT I DO WITH MY DAYS

WHAT I CURRENTLY LOOK LIKE

WHAT IS IMPORTANT RIGHT NOW

WHO I AM WRITING THIS FOR

WHAT I WANT TO GET OUT OF WRITING THIS

1

My Childhood

Whether your earliest memories consist of mostly schoolwork or a whole lot of play, of hardship or downtime, childhood is rife with rich content to mine and write about. In this section, we will explore young you—the before-adolescence you—capricious or cautious, loving or lonely. We will gather stories along the way and revisit fun events and big dreams. Your childhood might look different from other people's, and that's okay. Share as much as you are comfortable with, change questions to suit your liking, and come back to or skip questions that don't appeal to you at this moment. However you choose to approach this chapter, hold on tight and be ready to reflect: Your journey from birth through early childhood starts here.

PERHAPS YOUR NAME was passed down, or maybe it was merely popular at the time. What's the story behind your name?

MAYBE IT'S FUZZY or crystal clear, but go back as far as you can. What is your earliest memory?

WERE YOU OUTGOING or shy? An extrovert or an introvert? Write a quick story that illustrates why you identified as one or the other.

OUR APPEARANCES CAN change a lot over the years. What do you remember about the way you looked? What has stayed the same?

LET'S INVESTIGATE ONE of your "firsts." No event is too insignificant! The first tooth you lost, the first time you went to a friend's house, a first day of school—anything is fair game. Pick one and run wild with the memory.

OUR CLOSEST FRIENDS often come with our favorite traits. Who was your best friend as a kid, and what qualities did they have?

PETS CAN BE like family. Did you have pets? Which was your favorite? If you didn't have pets, what kind would have been ideal if you could have chosen one? Why?

CASTS, SPLINTS, OPERATIONS, oh my! It's hard to forget injuries. Did you ever have any accidents or break any bones as a kid?

THINGS THAT WE are afraid of—heights, snakes, clowns—we all have them. What were yours? Did you outgrow any of them?

WE SPEND MUCH of our childhood learning. Whether you went to school or were homeschooled, what do you recall about the physical space where you were taught?

THERE ARE ALWAYS certain academic subjects or extracurricular activities that we gravitate toward. Which did you like, and what was it about them that interested you?

THINK ABOUT A memorable teacher or two. What made them so impactful? Write what you remember most about them here.

DO YOU REMEMBER any dreams from when you were a kid? Maybe a nightmare? Or something reoccurring? If you don't remember any, what might you have dreamt about?

THE PLACES WE lived growing up can change the way we see the world. A "place" can be broad—such as a country, state, city, or township—or very narrow, like the room you shared with your sibling, for instance. Use these pages to dive in and write. Think about the smells, sights, feelings, and experiences you had there.

WHAT BOOK, MOVIE, or TV show made a big impact on you, and why do you think this was?

WHO WERE SOME of your favorite people? They could be neighbors, classmates, family, or someone else. What is a memorable occasion you shared with them?

THINGS AREN'T ALWAYS as they appear. What might people be surprised to learn about you from this period in your life?

WHEN YOU THINK about all of your childhood, what were the best things? What were the worst things?

LET'S GO BACK to the *very* beginning. What do you know about your birth, or perhaps adoption, story? What happened before, during, and after your birth? Include the time, place, and anything noteworthy. If there is anyone who can fill in the blanks, use this as an opportunity to interview them.

IT'S TIME FOR some fun! Write down all the toys, games, books, or activities you remember that kept you entertained as a kid.

KIDS DREAM OF many different possible careers. When you were small, what did you want to be when you grew up?

2

My Adolescence

As we get older, our world gets bigger. We meet more people and become exposed to more things. Perhaps we think more about our future, our world, and our place in it. This is the chapter for the slightly older, adolescent/teenage you. How did life change after early childhood? What remained the same? These pages offer you a chance to write down some of the fun stuff and, perhaps, delve deeper. As always, pen your story in whatever way feels right to you. If you have photos or memorabilia, I invite you to pull them out and sift through them, before and during your writing sessions. Maybe use the margins if new memories call to you. Go back, dig in, and explore it all!

THE THINGS WE engage in after (or before) school sometimes reveal our passions and callings. Sports, art, choir, debate—what were you interested in?

SOME OF US studied hard; others of us barely cracked a book. How did you do in school? Did this change from childhood?

IDOLS, CRUSHES, PEOPLE we admired . . . Whom did *you* look up to? What made them great in your eyes? Do they stand the test of time?

OFTEN ADOLESCENCE IS when we first establish, or break, our boundaries, and this may have led to fights with friends or others. Is there a particular conflict you remember? What happened?

WHETHER YOUR PARENTS or guardians were strict or not, it's common for teenagers to rebel in some way. What is the most rebellious thing you did as an adolescent?

ROMANCE. DEEP RESPECT. Even love. Did you first encounter it here? Did you have a significant other during this time or a significant relationship that sticks with you?

WHOM DID YOU spend the most time with during this stage? Did you have a group of friends? Were there people you wanted to be friends with?

FEELING AWKWARD IS often emblematic of youth. What is your most groan-worthy, embarrassing teen moment? Alternatively, what was your greatest moment of confidence?

TEEN YEARS OFTEN come with more responsibilities and independent experiences. What's one instance when you felt like an adult during this time? Maybe you were given car keys or stayed out later than you were supposed to. Pick a moment and remember it here.

IMPROMPTU OR COMPLETELY planned, what is a party or celebration you'll never forget? Who was there, and what made it memorable?

DESCRIBE WHERE YOU lived during this stage. If you lived in the same place since childhood, did your relationship to your home change as time went by?

HINDSIGHT IS 20/20, they say. What is one regret you have about this time? Is there anything that you would do differently?

WHAT DID YOU think your future would look like? Consider your hopes, dreams, and expectations. Were they realistic? Did things pan out? If not, would you even want them to?

WRITE "A DAY in the life" from your favorite adolescent age. You can try to remember a single day or take a bit of creative license and combine events together into one great day. If you have them, use journals or diaries as research materials. There's no wrong way; just have fun.

MUSIC CAN TRIGGER a million memories. What is one song, band, or group that takes you back? What do you think of? Alternatively, what other creative piece, such as a literary work, takes you back?

ONE'S "LOOK"—CLOTHING, hairstyle, etc.—can be the ultimate form of self-expression. Did you follow the trends or maintain a style all your own? Describe yours here.

DID YOU HAVE a job in high school? If you didn't have a job outside the home, were there chores or things to take care of at home?

SOMETIMES WE LEARN the easy way, but mistakes and missteps can also teach us a thing or two. What lessons did you learn during this time? From whom?

WRITE ABOUT SOMETHING that was "just yours" during this time. It could be your own room, a pet, maybe even a favorite piece of clothing. What did owning that item represent for you? Is there a story where that thing played a significant role?

LET'S REVISIT THE toys, games, books, or activities you liked and listed on page 16. What remained favorites as you became older? What new things kept you busy as a teen or young adult? List them here.

MEDALS AND ACHIEVEMENTS are great, but so are small wins and "firsts." What is an accomplishment of yours that has stuck with you?

3

Family Traditions and Memories

Families come in many shapes and sizes. Even mentioning the word "family" can elicit any number of reactions from people. Here is your chance to define family for yourself, as small or big or blended as it may be. I encourage you to change prompts or answer the questions in ways that suit your situation. The important part is to investigate your relationship to family, examine your traditions, and uncover and sift through old stories from the past. Perhaps family is just a set of values, or maybe you think of family as culture or heritage; there's a place to explore those ideas, too. However you show up on the page today, I wish you lots of "ahas," giggles, and maybe some therapeutic tears. Let's begin.

THINK ABOUT YOUR parents or people who played parental roles in your life. What are their names? What do you know about where they were born and their ancestry?

AT A PARTY, through mutual friends, by mistake . . . How did your parents or guardians meet? If you're not sure, how do you imagine they met?

WHAT ARE SOME defining traits of your siblings? If you didn't grow up with siblings, what was being an only child like?

WHO ARE YOU most similar to in your family? Consider aunts, uncles, and cousins, too. Who are you most different from? Who do you wish you were more like?

MANY FAMILIES HAVE narratives that have been passed down through generations, stories that are retold again and again. What's one of your family's tales? If you don't have a story like that in mind, maybe there's a story that you can pass down right now. Remember (or create) that infamous tale here.

WHAT ETHNICITY OR culture do you or your family identify with? How has this shaped you?

VALUES LIKE STRENGTH, loyalty, or freedom are often at the core of family units. What values did your family place importance on when you were growing up?

WRITE DOWN PLACES you went to as a family or as a child, including trips or nearby locales. If you didn't go many places, create a childhood sightseeing wish list.

SCENT IS PERHAPS the sense that can most effectively jog memory. Pick a family member and describe what they—or their home—smelled like.

WHAT RITUALS OR routines did your family have? An interesting greeting? Family hugs before bed? Identify one and write about it.

HOLIDAYS—RELIGIOUS OR cultural, widely known or even made up—are moments that often have lasting impact. What made them special or important to you or your family?

FOOD IS OFTEN a central component of family gatherings. What foods or meals did you eat growing up? Was there a particular dish that was special in your family?

WERE THERE PEOPLE you were so close to that they were almost family? An individual or even a group? Spend some time thinking and writing about them here.

IN YOUR MIND, what's at the heart of a family? You may think about parents, caregivers, or other forms of family—people you were close to growing up. Explore what qualities they had or those you wish they had. There's no wrong way to approach this. Simply take time to reflect and write your thoughts.

SOME FAMILIES PLAY sports together. Others are into the arts or nature. If you could define your family's "thing," what would that be?

GOOD OR BAD, what was a defining moment in your family? A birth, a death, a big event? What did that event mean to you?

WAS (OR IS) your family religious? How have your feelings about religion changed over the years? If your family wasn't religious, think about a belief or philosophy your family embraced.

MAYBE IT WAS a regular day, or perhaps something extraordinary happened. Write about a time when you felt close to your family.

THINK ABOUT YOUR time with your family as being on one long timeline. What big events stand out? You can list them out one by one or choose 5 to 10 happenings and devote a paragraph to each. Here is your chance to think linearly. Ready, set, write!

WHAT OBJECTS REMIND you of your family? They could be trinkets, heirlooms, souvenirs, hand-me-downs, or something else. Do you still have any of them?

DID YOU EVER have an illuminating moment with a loved one? Perhaps an unexpected conversation, a notable experience, or a time of surprising alliance? Reflect and write about the experience.

4

My Adult Life

As we shift out of childhood and adolescence, we turn now to look at you as an adult. The time from adolescence to now might be short, or perhaps it's been a while. As always, feel free to focus your writing on the time frame that you feel called to. This is the section to think about education: classes, training, college, military, experiences—anything that has influenced your perspective or deepened your understanding. And work life: Whether you've had many jobs outside the home or you are a stay-at-home mom or caregiver, we'll examine your thoughts on work. We will also uncover challenges, changes, opportunities, and aspirations during this time. There's a lot of material here to explore, so pick a place and plunge in!

GRADUATION, MOVING, MARRIAGE, loss, or maybe something else entirely—what is the biggest change you've experienced during this period of your life?

AS YOU WENT on to do new things, take chances, and perhaps experience new-found freedom as an adult, what person did you meet during this time whom you'll never forget?

WHAT IS ONE risk you took that you're most proud of? Maybe it made you nervous (or just everyone around you).

EDUCATION COMES IN a lot of different forms. What classes, training, or other types of education have you pursued?

THINK ABOUT YOURSELF at 18. What was your biggest dream or goal? Did it come true? In retrospect, is this a good or a bad thing?

THINK ABOUT SOMEWHERE you've driven, walked, biked, or traveled to. It doesn't have to be significant. Where were you going?

THINK ABOUT WHERE you've lived. Did you live with others or alone? Talk about your favorite room, apartment, house, or dwelling here.

WHAT IS SOMETHING you feel like you were really good at early in adulthood? Has this stayed the same? Have you become even better at it?

WHEN WE FIRST go out into the world on our own, the world can often present us with invitations to do new and exciting things. What opportunity changed your life for the better? Was it handed to you, was it luck, or did you work really hard for it? What other doors did that open?

PERHAPS VERY LITTLE (or a lot) irritates you. What annoyed you most early in adulthood? Would those things still affect you the same way today?

WRITE DOWN ALL the things you considered relaxing early in adulthood. Bonus if you can incorporate one or two back into your life.

IF SOMEONE HAD filmed a movie about your adulthood up till now, what would the plot synopsis and the title be? Who would play you?

WHAT IS THE most money you've ever earned? Was it worth it? What did you do with that money?

WHAT IS A misconception people have had about you? Or what was a misconception you've had about people or the world around you?

WHAT IS THE best or worst job you've had? Did you do it for very long? Alternatively, what job do you think is the best or worst in general?

WHAT DOES "WORK" mean to you? Is it following one's passion? Making a difference? Earning money? Explain your definition here. Has it changed over time?

FROM THE PEOPLE you've met to the places you've visited, what is something you want to remember from this period in your life?

FROM BABY BOOMERS to Gen Z, every group coming of age has unique world and societal issues they must contend with. What has been the biggest challenge people from your generation have faced? Has the issue changed over the years? If the issue hasn't been solved, what do you think needs to happen?

WE DON'T ALWAYS get it right, but we can learn from our pitfalls. What is a regret, mistake, or misstep you took as a young adult? What would you have done differently if you had the opportunity to do it over? How might life be different if you hadn't taken that road?

DOES YOUR CURRENT career or work (parenting counts!) match up with what you wanted to do or went to school for? If not, are you happy with your decision?

WHAT DO YOU consider the keys to successful "adulting," and what pearls of wisdom would you pass down on this grown-up subject?

5

A Few of My Favorite Things

When you learn a new language, it's not surprising that often many of the first phrases you learn begin with "I like . . . " Along with our values, hopes, and dreams, it's our preferences that define us. The combination of things we lean into—activities we do, places we frequent, things we consciously do with our free time—makes us unique. This chapter is perhaps the most entertaining because it's your chance to explore all of these: food you crave, art you admire, sports you enjoy, etc. There's even space for you to give advice to others, your own words of wisdom to help your family and friends learn about you and uncover their own favorite things. Let your fun side take the lead in this chapter!

WHAT'S THE BEST gift you have received or given yourself? Do you still have it? If it was a trip or experience, what do you remember about it?

WHETHER YOU ENJOY them often or infrequently, what are your luxuries, indulgences, or guilty pleasures? What makes them especially appealing?

PONDER YOUR FAVORITE pets since childhood. What makes them so amazing? If you've never had pets, what are some of your favorite animals and why?

WHAT CAUSE ARE you most passionate about? Was there an event or moment that connected you to it? How do you show your support? Volunteering, donating, or learning as much as you can?

WHAT'S YOUR FAVORITE season? What activities do you love to do during this time? What do you do in that season that you look forward to all year long? Are there holidays, events, or traditions that feature prominently? Write a memory about that time of year.

WHAT ARE SOME not-to-be-missed TV shows and movies in your world? Is there a specific type or theme that you gravitate toward? What makes them worth watching?

WHO ARE SOME of your favorite characters from books, films, TV, or even life? What makes them interesting, unique, or worth emulating?

WHAT IS YOUR favorite part of nature? What's the story behind how it came to mean something to you?

WHAT'S YOUR DRINK of choice? Soft drinks, coffee or tea, cocktail or mocktail? What is the sippable delight you can't live without?

THINK ABOUT YOUR favorite type of food. Do you eat it often or only occasionally? Have your favorites changed throughout the years? Is there anything you absolutely can't stand?

WHAT SMELL BRINGS to mind your favorite place? It could be somewhere you've been once or many times before. Think about your best time there and write about it.

WHAT'S YOUR FAVORITE musical genre and why? (We'll get more specific on songs and bands at the end of this chapter!)

RICH AND WARM or vivid and vibrant—how do your favorite colors work together or clash? What do you think this says about your personality?

WHETHER IN MUSEUMS, outdoors, online, or even your own creations, what are some of your favorite art pieces and why? Theater pieces, comedy routines, and performances count, too.

STORIES STICK WITH us, whether they're childhood fables, novels, movies, or poems. Write down all the books or stories that have stayed memorable for you over the years.

WHAT SPORTS DO you play or watch? Are you into a specific team or athlete? If you're not a player or die-hard fan, what can you appreciate about sports?

DID YOU DISCOVER your favorite things early in life? What advice would you give to others about finding the things they love?

WHAT ARE YOU most grateful for? It could be simple pleasures or basic needs, items, or activities. You'll get a chance in the next chapter to explore the people you love, but feel free to talk about them here as well, if you wish. However you approach this prompt, let your gratitude spill onto the page.

SOUND IS DIRECTLY linked to memory. Think about a song or band that you especially love. Has it always appealed to you? What emotions do you experience? What thoughts come back when you hear or remember this music or when you see this group perform? Write about a time when this music made its mark.

HOW WE SPEND our spare time says a lot about what we like. What hobbies, activities, or interests do you pursue in your downtime? Are there any new ones you'd like to try?

IF THERE ARE topics that didn't come up earlier in this chapter, here's your chance to list them. What are some other favorites of yours?

6

Friends and Loved Ones

Relationships make the world go round. Good friends and family members influence nearly everything we do. They help us be our best selves, celebrate our accomplishments, get us into trouble, and lead us into fun adventures.

Here, we'll consider relationships both short and long term, romantic and otherwise, people who have played leading and minor roles in your life. Maybe you'll write about an experience you haven't thought about in years. We will also gently ponder regrets, wrong turns, and things that didn't turn out as expected but may have left us better off. Suggestion: Write a list of those things you want to talk about and see if the prompts guide you there or somewhere else entirely. Wherever you go with this chapter, may it feel good to you.

IN THE CHILDHOOD chapter, you talked about your best friend. Outside of your family, who is your best friend now? Why do you think you are so close?

WITHIN YOUR FAMILY, who is the person you are closest to? How did this relationship evolve?

WHAT IS A question that you've always wanted to ask a friend or loved one but never asked? What do you imagine their response would be?

WHAT WAS YOUR first kiss like? Amazing or not so much? If you don't remember, what was an intimate moment with someone that comes to mind?

WHAT IS THE shortest relationship, romantic or otherwise, that you've ever had? What was a defining moment in that relationship?

WHAT IS THE longest relationship, romantic or otherwise, that you've ever had? What was a defining moment in that relationship?

WHAT IS THE most trouble you ever got in with a friend, significant other, acquaintance, or relative? Did you get away with it? Were there serious ramifications?

LIST SOME OF the dates you've gone on or some of the wild adventures you've had with your closest friends. Explore them here.

YOU'RE A CHEF, and you need to compile ingredients. What is the recipe for an enduring romantic relationship? Or a lasting friendship? Is it dedication, trust, and maybe a healthy dose of humor? What's the right balance? Are there steps to the relationship-building process? Reflect on a person who embodies all (or most) of the necessary ingredients and write the recipe.

IF WE'RE LUCKY, we have cheerleaders, those people who support us no matter what. Who is/are yours? How do they show you their support?

THINK ABOUT A partnership you've been in, romantic or otherwise. What is/was your favorite thing about this person? Do you have a fun story to illustrate this?

DO YOU HAVE an unusual or funny way that you met a close friend? Did they approach you or did you approach them? What happened?

THE GRASS IS always greener, they say. Which loved one's life is so interesting or enviable that you would switch places with them for the day?

HAVE YOU EVER met a celebrity? Share that story here. If you haven't, who would you love to meet and why?

WHICH FRIENDSHIP OR relationship did you have that you can't believe you had? What did you learn from it?

OLDER OR YOUNGER friends and those of different generations can offer completely different perspectives. What has an ally, companion, or colleague of a different age taught you?

THE NURSE IN the hospital, the person who sat in front of you in a class in college . . . Who has made brief cameos in your life that you still remember?

WHETHER IT WAS mind-blowing or a complete disaster, what is the best or worst date you've ever been on? Use the list prompt on page 95 to help you pick and elaborate more on it here. If you haven't really dated, focus on the best or worst outing, activity, or event you've attended with a friend or colleague.

WRITE ABOUT ONE impactful relationship that you've only touched on in previous prompts or haven't yet explored. How did you meet? What makes that dynamic so special? What are some things you never want to forget about this person? What have you overcome?

THINK OF SOMETHING you haven't written about yet. What is one (good or bad) memory with a close friend, family member, or significant other that you'll never forget?

WHAT IS A phrase, proverb, or saying about relationships that you strongly agree with? Alternatively, what is the best advice you have received about relationships?

My Community

Sometimes, it's intentional; other times, it's luck of the draw. When we come together, it can be an amazing thing. The size of the group, team, or organization means little. With common goals, it's incredible what people can accomplish. Groups provide support, comfort, and safety—truth is, we need each other. We are social creatures; it's natural for us to seek each other out and experience the world and the people in it. Here is the place to talk about communities: not only the good ones, but those that could have functioned better, too. Digging down, you'll consider what communities need to thrive. It's a big topic, so start slow, fill out those prompts you most gravitate toward first, and enjoy exploring all that this chapter unearths.

WHERE DO YOU currently live? Small town or big city? What is your relationship like with those who live in your vicinity?

COMPARE YOUR CURRENT community or neighborhood with those from your past. How have your surroundings differed, changed, or remained the same?

WHETHER IN MARCHING bands, book clubs, and anything in between, who are the people you've participated in activities with? What is a challenging or memorable moment you experienced with them?

SOME PEOPLE ARE closer to their neighbors than others. But whether you knew a lot about them or very little, try to record those neighbors you remember here.

ARE THERE PLACES or businesses you frequent that you feel a bond with? Why do you gravitate toward them?

WHERE DO YOU seek news or entertainment? Is there a station or person you turn to? Why are they the ones you go to?

WHAT ARE SOME groups, families, or cultures that you admire? What facets of their connection stand out to you? What is their strength or "superpower"?

DO YOU HAVE workplace colleagues or people you participated in a project with who come to mind? Talk about what you accomplished—or what went wrong—in this space.

WHEN IS A time you truly felt connected to others you didn't know? Perhaps it was through a shared societal event, like 9/11 or the COVID-19 pandemic. How did this event change your perception of others? Do you still feel that way? Reflect on that time and what you took away from it.

NOT ALL CONNECTIONS come to fruition. Whether in school, your neighborhood, or another community, when is a time that you felt you didn't belong?

WHAT'S A GROUP you wanted to join but didn't? Perhaps you were afraid, or the timing wasn't right. Alternatively, if you could form a group, what would it be? What qualities would be important?

PROVIDING MENTORSHIP CAN be as fulfilling as receiving it. Do you have a mentee? Or who can you imagine might look up to you?

WE SEE THEM in the media all the time: close-knit circles of friends who do everything together. Have you ever had a small group of really good friends? Or do you prefer larger, looser groups?

IT'S THE TOPIC that fires us up: politics. Have you ever campaigned for a cause or run for an office or leadership role? Whether you have been involved or not, whether you are independent or affiliated, what are your thoughts about government (on any level)? Investigate your viewpoint here.

THINK ABOUT VOWS, promises, or oaths you may have taken, either with others or as an individual. They could be during a marriage, religious, or initiation ceremony or just words you live by. Whatever the case, which vows hold the most meaning? Which are outdated or no longer appeal to you?

WHAT SPECIFICS DO you remember about your schools? Were there a lot of students? A mascot? What was important or interesting about each school's culture?

WHAT PARTS OF society have always exasperated you? Laws, norms, injustices? What are one or two things you disagree with? What would you change?

WHAT GROUPS, ORGANIZATIONS, clubs, or causes have you belonged to or supported? Make a list here.

WHAT IS THE best way to break away from a group? Have you ever had to do this? If not, think about some dealbreakers that might make you want to.

ROLE MODELS OR mentors can be pivotal in shaping our careers and lives. Who are yours? Who is someone famous that would make a good one?

NOW FOR YOUR wisdom. What advice would you give to others for building strong communities?

8

My Life as a Mother

Maybe you always wanted to be a mother; maybe life just flowed along or it happened unexpectedly. This section is for every type of mother: those who became a mom through birth, adoption, fostering, or surrogacy and those who became guardians in other ways. Welcome, all. Perhaps you're a stepparent, grandparent, or other relative or the mother figure to a child or children. Heterosexual, same-sex, single parents—there's no one way to do it. Every story is different, but regardless of how you became a mom or what your family unit looks like, becoming a mother is often life changing. Here is the chapter to bring pen to paper with your own unique story. Before you get into it, though, show yourself some appreciation for doing this rewarding, hard, often invisible, and oh-so-important work of motherhood.

THINK BACK TO the moment you knew you would be a parent. How did you feel? Whom did you tell first?

WHAT IS YOUR parenting style? Perhaps you are strict or more go with the flow. Has your style changed? Is it the same as the way you grew up?

WHAT IS A "first" you will always remember with your kid or kids? Maybe it makes you smile, laugh, or even cry.

WORDS THEY SAY, funny things they do . . . List all the unique things that you never want to forget about your kid or kids.

WHETHER IT WAS your body, time spent on friendships, or other things, how do you feel your life changed when you became a mother?

WHETHER IT'S SLEEPING in or being a bit wild, is there anything you miss about life before kids?

WE ALL HAVE people we look up to. They may be in our life or well-known public figures. Who are your parenting role models that you turn to for advice or support? Why?

WHAT ARE THE predominant messages you receive about parenting and motherhood from your culture, society, or circle of friends? What do you appreciate? What needs updating?

WHAT DO YOU see as the biggest misconception about motherhood? How did your vision of motherhood match up with the real thing?

WHAT'S YOUR FAVORITE part about being a mother or parenting? Let your mind roam a bit before responding.

AS MOTHERS, WE all have struggles. What are some of your parental struggles? How have you dealt with them?

BESIDES THOSE IN your immediate family, who are some other people that have a big impact on your kid's or kids' lives?

LET'S THINK BACK to the beginning of your motherhood experience. Use this space to pen your kid's or kids' birth, adoption, foster, or surrogacy story. Start and end the story wherever you'd like. If it was a difficult period, include that, if you're comfortable doing so. What was meaningful about that time?

LET'S CAPTURE THE present moment right now! Close your eyes. What does your child or children look like? What does their laugh sound like? Note the details.

YOU'VE THOUGHT ABOUT what your kid or kids look like; now let's document what they are "into" at the moment. Books, games, stories, TV shows, activities, etc.—write them all down.

DESCRIBE YOUR CHILD or children in one word. Perhaps you have a story to illustrate why you chose that word. Tell it below.

WHAT IS SOMETHING you appreciate about this stage in your kid's or kids' lives? What is something you're looking forward to in the next stage?

TIME TO BREAK out the tissues! Write a letter to your child or children. You can include any of the observations from previous prompts or just lay out all your hopes and wishes for them. You might choose to date the letter and ask that they open it then. Or maybe this is just for you.

REFLECT ON A favorite memory with your child or children. It could be a regular day or a special event. Where were you and what were you doing? Why does this particular time have meaning? Consider both the big picture and the small details as you write.

PARENTING INCLUDES A lot of learning on the fly. Knowing what you do now, what would you do differently if you got to redo the past few years with your kid or kids?

WHAT ARE SOME pieces of advice you have for new moms (or maybe for your child or children when/if they have kids of their own)?

9

My Future Dreams

Sometimes revisiting the past can be overwhelming, but hopefully you feel inspired by the many things you've done, experienced, and accomplished so far. "My Future Dreams" is all about that: you and what you envision for the future. This is the place to figure out what you want down the road. How would you like to develop or improve? What goals do you want to accomplish? Whom do you want to meet? You can answer any of these prompts with a general time frame in mind, or for more specificity, I encourage you to assign months or years to them. For instance, add "in a year" or "in five years" to any prompt, if you think that's helpful. However you approach this section, best wishes as you journey onward!

WHAT INSPIRES YOU when you look toward the future? It might be something that helps you get out of bed each day or just a random happy thought.

WHO ARE SOME people you hope to meet or reconnect with? It could be someone famous, a coworker from the past, or your soulmate. Why?

WHAT IS ONE bad habit you would like to kick in the future?

THINK MORE ABSTRACTLY here about other things you might like to change. What fears, negative behaviors, or ideas would you like to let go of?

ONE THING IS certain: nothing stays the same. What is the biggest change you see for yourself and your family in the time ahead?

DO YOU SEE yourself staying where you are or moving? If you go somewhere, will it be far? How might your living situation change in the years to come?

WE ALL WANT our loved ones to have amazing lives. What is one wish you have for your community, family, and/or friends?

IF YOU THINK about right now, tomorrow, or next week, what is something joyful or fun that you can incorporate into your upcoming days?

EARLIER, YOU WERE asked to describe a day from your youth (page 28). Now let's imagine a day yet to come. Describe in detail a day from your life 10 years from now. Where are you? Who are you with? What are you doing? How do you feel? Remember to include all five senses!

MAYBE THERE ARE family trips you want to take or things you'd like to do together. What are some things you hope to see or experience with your family?

IF YOU HAVE any roadblocks ahead, list them here. What do you think stands in the way of your ideal future?

PRETEND ALL YOUR roadblocks are diminished. What will your ideal life look like? What is happiness in your future?

LET'S GET SCI-FI for a minute. What medical or technological advances are you most hoping to see in the future?

IS THERE ANYTHING else you would like to see come to fruition? What about societally or globally? What else needs to change?

WHAT LEGACY WOULD you like to leave for your family? What do you want your family or friends to remember most about you?

WHAT IS ONE place you absolutely must visit? Describe your trip. Or write about several places, then circle the ones you might visit in the next two years.

IF YOU DON'T have them already, what might it look like to have grandchildren? If you do, what do you imagine for them?

LET'S IMAGINE YOU, years from now, hopefully a little wiser and maybe feeling more authentically *you*. How would your "future self" model the way for your current self? What advice can this wise version of yourself give? What pieces of comfort can they offer to you now?

SKIP AHEAD TO the next prompt and fill out your list of goals. Then come back here and expand on one. Here's your place to break it into smaller steps. How will you get there? What will it feel like once you've achieved it? Be as specific as possible.

LIST ALL THE personal and/or professional goals you have for yourself here. They can be very small and simple or wild and audacious.

IF THERE ARE other things about the future that you'd like to ruminate on, this is the place. What else do you want to include here to remember going forward?

ACKNOWLEDGMENTS

Mom, my first book was dedicated to you, but without you, none of the others would be possible. Patty and Paul, thank you for all you do and for raising Joey—the best partner and co-parent I could ask for. For Declan: You'll never know how much I love you, but I will forever try to show you. For Vanessa Putt, Eun H. Jeong, and everyone else at Callisto: I truly love working with you.

Judy Reeves and Jill Hall, this one is for you. Thank you for introducing me to the eye-opening world of prompt writing and for your unwavering support and generosity, particularly during this past year and a half. I am so thankful for you both.

ABOUT THE AUTHOR

KRISTEN FOGLE has been the executive director of San Diego Writers, Ink, a nonprofit literary center, since 2013. She's also a writing instructor, teaching artist, and theatrical producer, director, and performer. Find out more at KristenFogle.com or SanDiegoWriters.org.

CPSIA information can be obtained
at www.ICGtesting.com
Printed in the USA
JSHW022101140222
22843JS00001B/1

9 781638 073642